Explanatory

Grades 4–6

Project Manager:
Elizabeth H. Lindsay

Writer:
Stephanie Willett-Smith

Contributing Editor:
Cayce Guiliano

Art Coordinator:
Clevell Harris

Artists:
Pam Crane, Teresa R. Davidson, Clevell Harris, Rob Mayworth,
Barry Slate, Donna K. Teal

Cover Artists:
Nick Greenwood and Kimberly Richard

Writing Works!

www.themailbox.com

Manufactured in the United States
10 9 8 7 6 5 4 3 2 1

Table of Contents

About This Book

What Is Explanatory Writing?

In *explanatory writing*, a writer tells or explains how to do something. The writer uses transitional or linking words, such as *first, next, then,* and *finally* to help the reader understand the order of the steps in the explanation.

Develop and enhance your students' explanatory-writing skills with this easy-to-use collection of 20 two-page lessons. *Writing Works!—Explanatory* contains everything you need to supplement a successful writing program in your classroom.

Each two-page lesson contains the following:

- A motivating writing prompt
- Simple steps for teaching the prewriting and writing stages of each lesson
- A student reproducible that is either a graphic organizer used in the prewriting stages or a pattern on which students write their final drafts
- Suggestions for publishing or displaying students' work

Also included:

- A reproducible proofreading checklist for the student
- A reproducible explanatory-writing assessment for the teacher
- 16 extra explanatory-writing prompts
- A student reproducible containing 13 commonly used editing symbols

Other books in the Writing Works! series:

- *Writing Works!—Descriptive*
- *Writing Works!—Narrative*
- *Writing Works!—Clarification*
- *Writing Works!—Persuasive*
- *Writing Works!—Expressive*

Sandwich Spectacular!

PROMPT *Think about your favorite type of sandwich. Then write a paragraph explaining how to make this sandwich so someone who has never made it before can do this.*

Think It!

1. Explain to students how to make a glass of chocolate milk. Be very detailed in your explanation, and use transitional or linking words as you describe the steps. Next have student volunteers recall the steps, giving specific words or phrases that helped them remember the order.

2. Have each student visualize his favorite sandwich, thinking about the ingredients and the steps needed to make it.

3. Read aloud the prompt above, display it on a transparency, or write it on the board. Then give each student a copy of page 5.

4. Instruct each student to write all of the steps needed to make his favorite sandwich on the organizer at the top of page 5. Then direct him to number the steps in the correct order.

Write It!

1. On another sheet of paper, have the student use the information recorded at the top of page 5 to write a paragraph about how to make his sandwich. Remind the student that he is writing to explain and should use transitional or linking words similar to those you used in your example. Also remind him to include a topic sentence and a concluding sentence in his paragraph.

2. Direct the student to proofread and edit his work carefully. Encourage students to swap papers to peer-edit.

3. After all corrections have been made, instruct each student to write his final copy on the sandwich pattern on the bottom of page 5.

4. If desired, have each student cut out his sandwich pattern. Then display the completed patterns on a bulletin board titled "No Matter How You Slice It, Our Sandwiches Are Spectacular!"

Sandwich Spectacular!

Step ———	
Step ———	
Step ———	
Step ———	
Step ———	
Step ———	

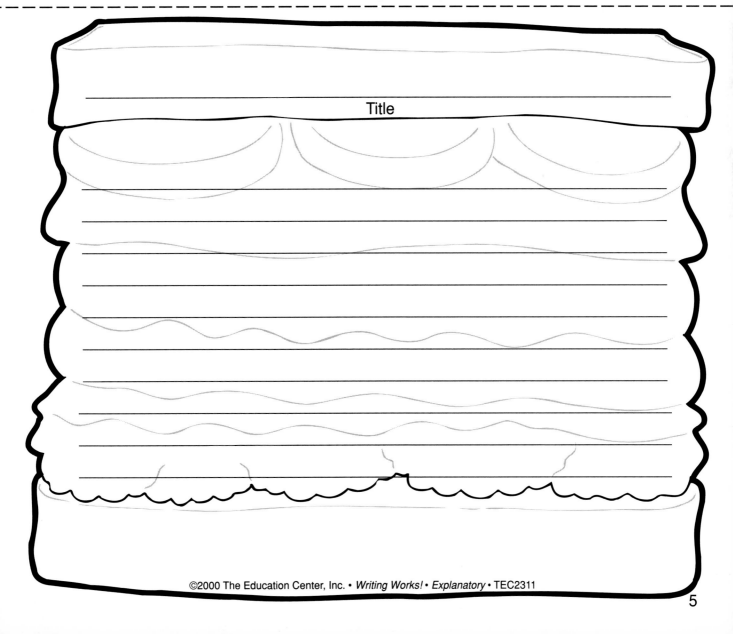

Title

Just Plane Directions!

PROMPT

Think about the last time you made a paper airplane, how you made it, and how well it flew. Write a paragraph explaining how to make a paper airplane from a sheet of loose-leaf paper.

Think It!

1. Have each student take out a sheet of loose-leaf paper. Challenge each student to make a paper airplane from the sheet. Encourage the student to pay close attention to each step as she creates the plane.

2. Read aloud the prompt above, display it on a transparency, or write it on the board. Then give each student a copy of page 7.

3. Instruct each student to use the spaces provided on the reproducible to sketch the steps she followed to make her paper airplane. Encourage the student to make another plane as she draws, if necessary. Direct the student to draw more boxes on the back of the page, if needed.

4. Below each sketch, have the student write a sentence explaining that step.

Write It!

1. On another sheet of paper, have the student use the information recorded on page 7 to write a paragraph, including a topic sentence and a concluding sentence. Remind the student that she is writing to explain and should use transitional or linking words to make the steps easier to follow.

2. Direct the student to proofread and edit her work carefully. Encourage students to swap papers to peer-edit. After all corrections have been made, have the student write her final copy on another sheet of paper.

3. After writing her final copy, have the student exchange paragraphs with a classmate and follow the directions as written to make a paper airplane. Then take students outside to test the planes. If desired, display planes and final copies on a bulletin board titled "Just Plane Directions!"

Just Plane Directions!

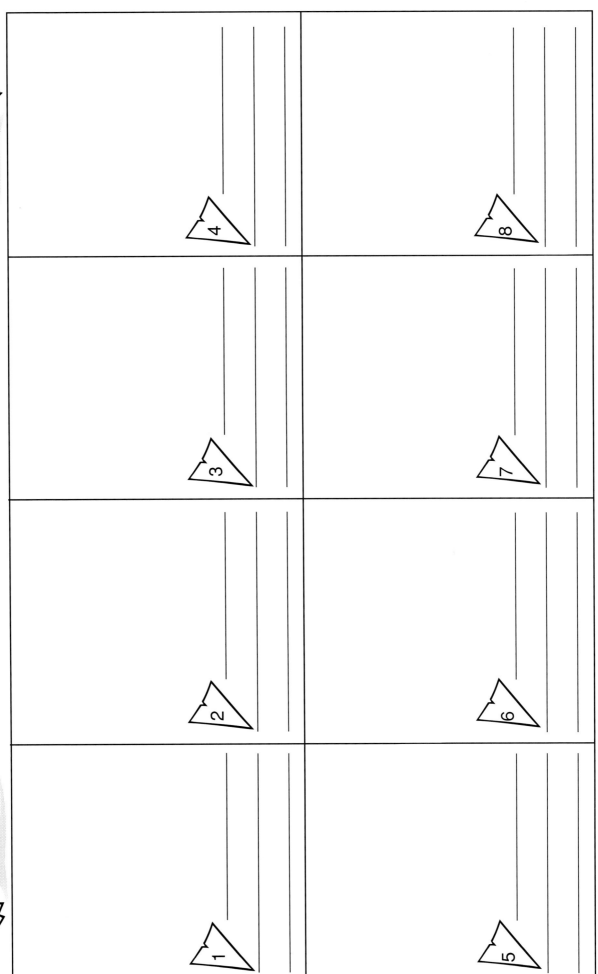

Treasure Trek

Imagine that a treasure is discovered hidden somewhere in your school and you are the only one who knows where it is. Write a paragraph explaining how to find the treasure.

Think It!

1. Draw a rough sketch of your school on the board. Then explain how to get from your classroom to another area of the school, using the sketch you drew. As you explain, be sure to use transitional and linking words, as well as directional words, to help students understand your instructions.

2. Read aloud the prompt above, display it on a transparency, or write it on the board.

3. Have each student use the map you drew on the board to select a location in the school for the hidden treasure. Then give each student a copy of page 9 and instruct him to draw his own map of the school, including a key or legend.

Write It!

1. On another sheet of paper, have the student write a paragraph giving directions for finding the hidden treasure. Remind him that he is writing to explain and should use transitional or linking words. Also remind him to include a topic sentence and a concluding sentence in his paragraph.

2. Direct the student to proofread and edit his work carefully. Encourage students to swap papers to peer-edit.

3. After all corrections have been made, instruct each student to write his final copy on the bottom of page 9.

4. If desired, have students exchange papers and go on a treasure hunt to check the directions. Display students' maps and final copies on a bulletin board titled "Our Treasure Trek!"

Treasure Trek

School Treasure Map

Map Key

©2000 The Education Center, Inc. • *Writing Works!* • *Explanatory* • TEC2311

_____

(Title)

Crafty Creations

PROMPT

Think about your favorite arts-and-crafts project. Write one or more paragraphs explaining how to make this project so a friend could make it too!

Think It!

1. Share with students an arts-and-crafts project that you or someone you know has created. Explain the steps for making this project. Examples may include crocheting an afghan or building a model.

2. Ask student volunteers to describe arts-and-crafts projects they have made or seen someone else make. List the projects on the board.

3. Read aloud the prompt above, display it on a transparency, or write it on the board. Then give each student a copy of page 11.

4. In the space provided, instruct each student to list the supplies needed to complete her project. Challenge the student to use the list she made to help her explain the steps needed to make her project.

Write It!

1. Instruct each student to use the information recorded on page 11 to write one or more paragraphs on another sheet of paper. Remind her that she is writing to explain and should use transitional or linking words. Also remind her to include a topic sentence and a concluding sentence in her paragraph(s).

2. Direct the student to proofread and edit her work carefully. Encourage students to swap papers to peer-edit. After all corrections have been made, have the student write her final draft on a separate sheet of paper.

3. If desired, combine all of the final copies into a class book titled "Our Class's Crafty Creations!"

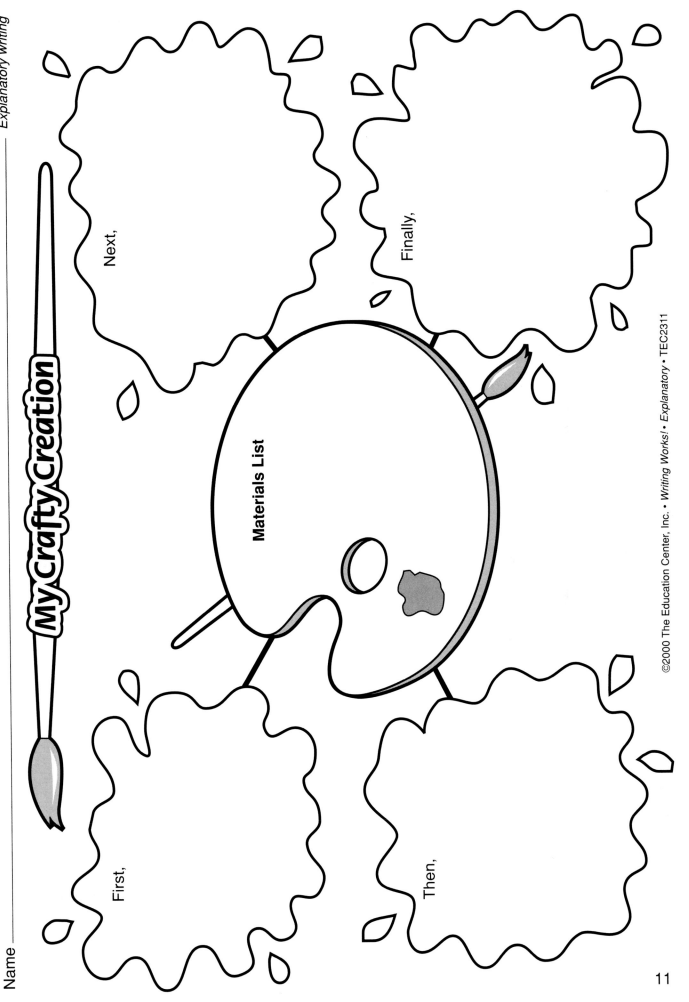

My Crafty Creation

Next,

Finally,

Materials List

First,

Then,

Critter Sitters

PROMPT

Imagine you are going out of town for a weekend and have asked a friend to care for your pet while you're gone. Write one or more paragraphs to your friend, explaining how to care for your pet.

Think It!

1. Ask a student volunteer to share a time when he was asked to care for a pet. On the board, list the tasks or types of things the student did to care for the pet.

2. Read aloud the prompt above, display it on a transparency, or write it on the board. Then give each student a copy of page 13.

3. Have each student choose a real or imaginary pet he would like his friend to care for while he is gone. Have the student draw a picture of the pet in the first box.

4. In the second box, have the student list the animal's needs and supplies, such as food, exercise, and shelter.

5. In the last box on page 13, have the student write the steps explaining how to care for his pet.

Write It!

1. On another sheet of paper, have the student use the information recorded on page 13 to write detailed pet care instructions for his friend. Remind the student that he is writing to explain and should use transitional or linking words. Also remind him to include a topic sentence and a concluding sentence in his paragraph(s).

2. Direct the student to proofread and edit his work carefully. Encourage students to swap papers to peer-edit. After all corrections have been made, instruct the student to write his final copy on a separate sheet of paper.

3. If desired, display students' final copies on a bulletin board covered in newspaper titled "Critter Sitters!"

Name ____________________

Critter Sitters

MY PET

NEEDS AND SUPPLIES

______________________ ______________________
______________________ ______________________
______________________ ______________________
______________________ ______________________
______________________ ______________________
______________________ ______________________

PET CARE INSTRUCTIONS

First, ____
____
____

Next, ____
____
____

Then, ____
____
____

Finally, ____
____
____

Drop Me a Line!

PROMPT *Imagine that your best friend has moved. You both have decided to write friendly letters to one another, but she doesn't know how. Write a paragraph explaining how to write a friendly letter so your friend can write to you.*

Think It!

1. As a class, write a friendly letter to someone in your school, such as another teacher, the custodian, or the secretary. Write the letter on the board. Then, with your students' help, point out the parts of the letter—*heading, greeting, body, closing,* and *signature.* Write them on the board next to their matching letter parts.

2. Read aloud the prompt above, display it on a transparency, or write it on the board. Then give each student a copy of page 15.

3. On the envelope at the top of the page, have the student list the steps for writing a friendly letter. Instruct the student to not only identify the parts of a friendly letter in her steps, but to also give details about what each part includes. For example, in the heading of a friendly letter, be sure to include the sender's address and the date.

Write It!

1. On another sheet of paper, have each student use the information recorded on the reproducible to write a paragraph explaining how to write a friendly letter. Remind the student that she is writing to explain and should use transitional or linking words. Also remind the student to include a topic sentence and a concluding sentence in her paragraph.

2. Direct the student to proofread and edit her work carefully. Encourage students to swap papers to peer-edit.

3. After all corrections have been made, have each student write her final copy on the letter outline on page 15.

4. If desired, instruct students to cut out their final copies. Then give each student an envelope and have her address it to her friend. Display the letters and envelopes on a bulletin board titled "Drop Me a Line!"

Name ____________________

Drop Me a Line!

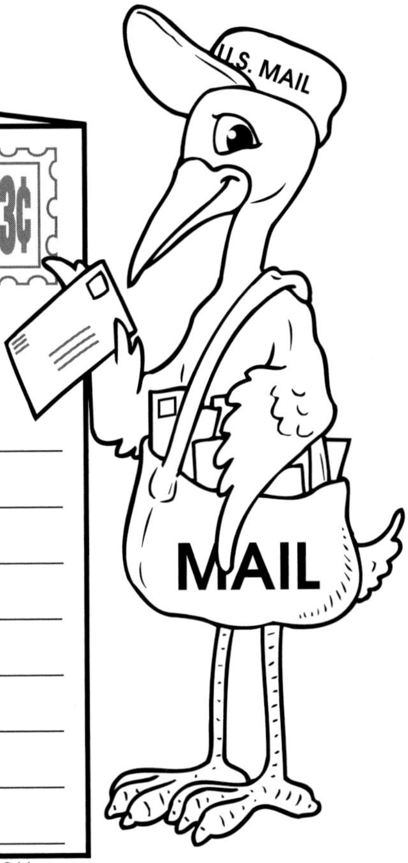

Steps for Writing a Friendly Letter

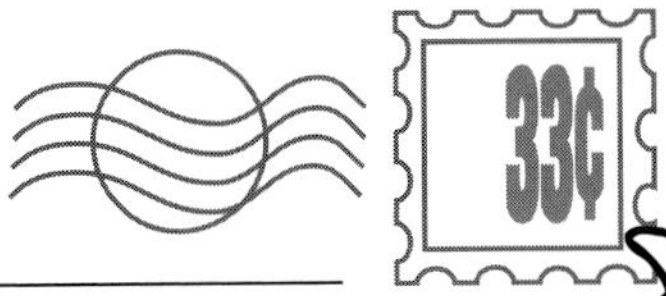

First, ____________________

____

Next, ____________________

____

Then, ____________________

____

Finally, ____________________

____

____

(Title)

____

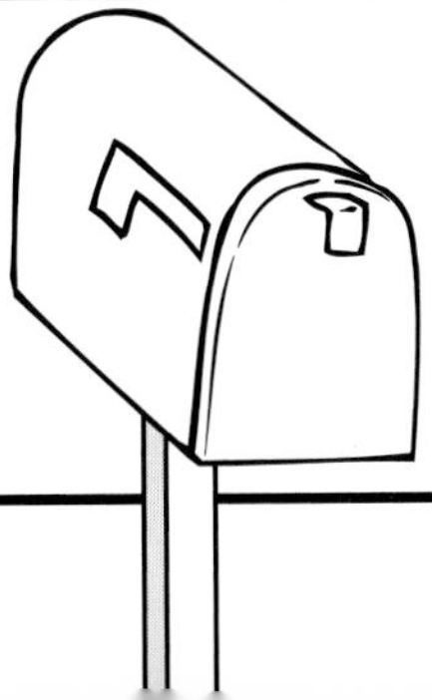

©2000 The Education Center, Inc. • *Writing Works!* • *Explanatory* • TEC2311

Snack to It!

PROMPT *Imagine you are getting ready for an upcoming sleepover at your house. You want your mom to make your favorite snack for you and your friends. Write a paragraph for your mom explaining how to make the snack.*

Think It!

1. Ask students to imagine what would happen if a baker iced a cake before he put it in the oven or a butcher wrapped up meat before he cut it. Brainstorm with students other activities in which following sequential directions is important.

2. Read aloud the prompt above, display it on a transparency, or write it on the board.

3. Give each student a copy of page 17. Direct the student to list all of the ingredients and supplies he will need on the recipe card at the top of the page.

4. At the bottom of the page, have the student write the steps needed to make his snack. Encourage the student to include serving suggestions, such as serves four people, place in a bowl with the crackers on the side, or arrange so the colors alternate.

Write It!

1. On another sheet of paper, have the student use the information recorded on page 17 to write a paragraph giving instructions on how to make his favorite snack. Remind the student that he is writing to explain and should use transitional or linking words. Also remind him to include a topic sentence and a concluding sentence in his paragraph.

2. Direct the student to proofread and edit his work carefully. Encourage students to swap papers to peer-edit.

3. After all corrections have been made, instruct each student to write his final copy on a recipe card made from half of a file folder. If desired, create a class recipe book titled "Snack to It!"

Name ____________________

Snack to It!

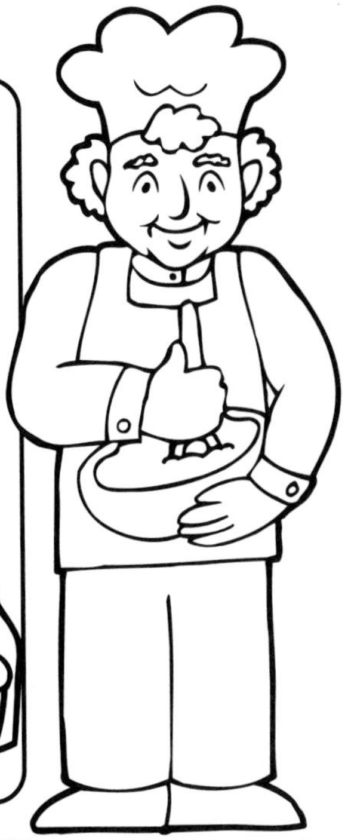

My Favorite Snack ____________________

Ingredients and Supplies

____

____

____

____

____

____

____

____

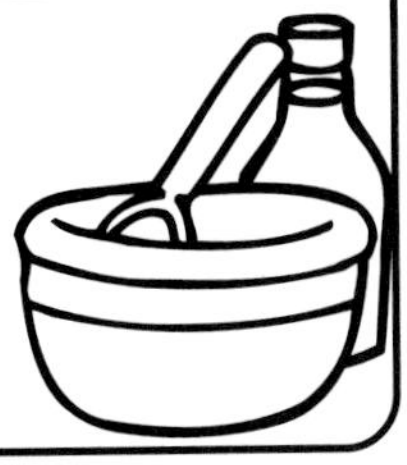

Steps for
Making My Snack

First, ____________________

____

____

Next, ____________________

____

____

Then, ____________________

____

____

Finally, ____________________

____

____

Planning the Perfect Party

PROMPT *Imagine that your birthday is next week. Write one or more paragraphs to your parents explaining how to plan the perfect birthday party.*

Think It!

1. Ask students to imagine what a perfect birthday party would be like. Then have student volunteers share their ideas with the class.

2. Help students brainstorm the types of things that would help make a party a success. For example, a student might suggest invitations, decorations, games, and refreshments. Write student suggestions on the board.

3. Read aloud the prompt above, display it on a transparency, or write it on the board.

4. Give each student a copy of page 19. Have the student list the supplies and explain the steps needed to prepare for her perfect party.

Write It!

1. On another sheet of paper, have the student use the information recorded on page 19 to write instructions for her parents on how to plan the perfect party. Remind her that she is writing to explain and should use transitional or linking words. Also remind her to include a topic sentence and a concluding sentence in her paragraph(s).

2. Direct the student to proofread and edit her work carefully. Encourage students to swap papers to peer-edit.

3. After all corrections have been made, give each student a sheet of light-colored construction paper on which to draw and cut out a large balloon. Then have the student write her final copy on the balloon cutout.

4. If desired, display students' final copies on a bulletin board titled "Planning the Perfect Party!"

Planning the Perfect Party

Then,

Finally,

Next,

Supplies:

First,

It's All Fun and Games!

PROMPT *Think about your favorite inside game and how it is played. Write one or more paragraphs explaining the directions for this game so your best friend will be able to play it with you.*

rattle rattle

Think It!

1. Ask students to think about a time when they played an inside game that was new to them, such as dominoes, checkers, or a board game. Point out the importance of having directions, whether written or verbal, to learn the rules of a new game.

2. Read aloud the prompt above, display it on a transparency, or write it on the board. Then give each student a copy of page 21.

3. Direct each student to use the top of page 21 to list the materials needed to play his favorite game. Then have the student think about the steps required to play his game. Challenge him to list these steps in the space provided.

4. Have the student read over his directions and number them in the order in which they should be followed.

Write It!

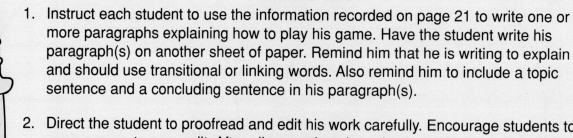

1. Instruct each student to use the information recorded on page 21 to write one or more paragraphs explaining how to play his game. Have the student write his paragraph(s) on another sheet of paper. Remind him that he is writing to explain and should use transitional or linking words. Also remind him to include a topic sentence and a concluding sentence in his paragraph(s).

2. Direct the student to proofread and edit his work carefully. Encourage students to swap papers to peer-edit. After all corrections have been made, have the student write his final copy on another sheet of paper.

3. If desired, place each student's directions in a folder labeled with the title of his game. Allow students to bring in their favorite games from home. Place the folders and games at a center. Have students select a game to test and play with a classmate during free time.

It's All Fun and Games!

Game Materials

_____   _____

_____   _____

_____   _____

_____   _____

Steps to Play My Game

☐ _____

☐ _____

☐ _____

☐ _____

☐ _____

☐ _____

☐ _____

☐ _____

☐ _____

Be My Valentine!

PROMPT *Imagine that your friend wants your help designing a unique valentine for a special person. Write a paragraph to your friend explaining how to make this valentine.*

Think It!

1. Ask students to recall the last valentine they can remember giving or receiving. Have student volunteers explain whether they prefer getting store-bought valentines or those made by hand and why.

2. Read aloud the prompt above, display it on a transparency, or write it on the board. Then give each student a copy of page 23.

3. In the space provided, have each student list the materials needed to make her valentine (for example, construction paper, glue, glitter, and scissors).

4. On the bottom of page 23, have the student use her materials list to write the steps required to make her valentine.

You're Special!

Write It!

1. Direct each student to write a paragraph on another sheet of paper using the information recorded on page 23. Remind the student that she is writing to explain and should use transitional or linking words. Also remind her to include a topic sentence and a concluding sentence in her paragraph.

2. Direct the student to proofread and edit her work carefully. Encourage students to peer-edit. After all corrections have been made, have the student write her final copy on another sheet of paper.

3. If desired, have each student trade papers with a classmate to test her directions. Display directions and completed valentines by using a length of yarn to tie them together. Then hang them from the ceiling and title your display "Be My Valentine!"

Be My Valentine!

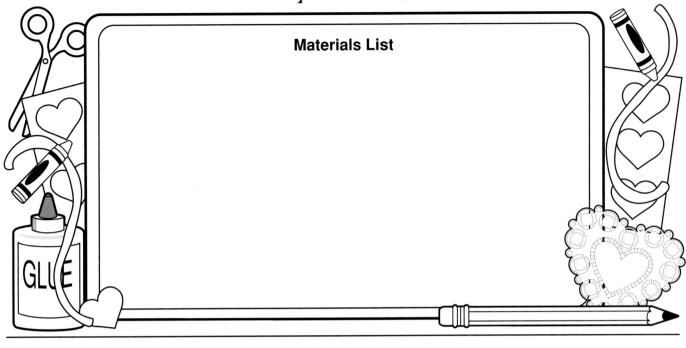

Materials List

First, _____
_____
_____

Next, _____
_____

Then, _____
_____

Finally, _____
_____

Order Up!

PROMPT

Imagine that a visitor from another country is staying with your family. You want to take him to a fast-food restaurant, but he has never been to one. Write a paragraph for the visitor explaining how to order a meal in a fast-food restaurant.

Think It!

1. Instruct each student to close his eyes and think about the last time he went to a fast-food restaurant. Have him retrace his steps from the time he entered the restaurant until the time he was served his food.

2. Ask student volunteers to share their experiences with the class.

3. Read aloud the prompt above, display it on a transparency, or write it on the board. Then give each student a copy of page 25.

4. At the top of page 25, have each student write the steps a person must follow to order a meal in a fast-food restaurant.

Write It!

1. On a sheet of paper, have the student write a paragraph explaining how to order a fast-food meal using the information recorded on page 25. Remind him to use transitional or linking words and to include a topic sentence and a concluding sentence.

2. Direct the student to proofread and edit his work carefully. Encourage students to swap papers to peer-edit.

3. After all corrections have been made, have the student write his final copy on the hamburger pattern at the bottom of page 25.

4. If desired, have each student cut out his completed paragraph and display it on a bulletin board titled "Order Up!"

Order Up!

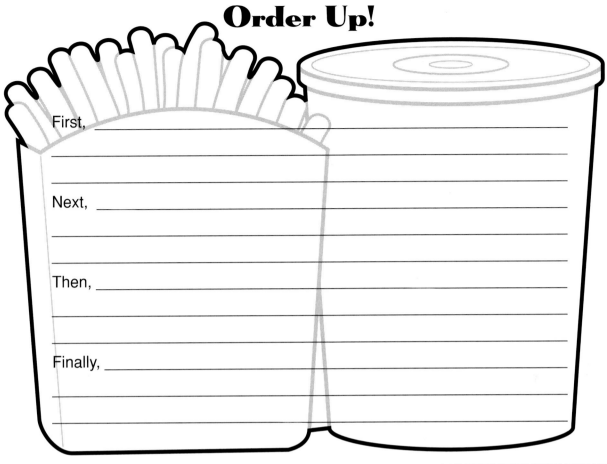

First, _____
_____

Next, _____
_____

Then, _____
_____

Finally, _____
_____

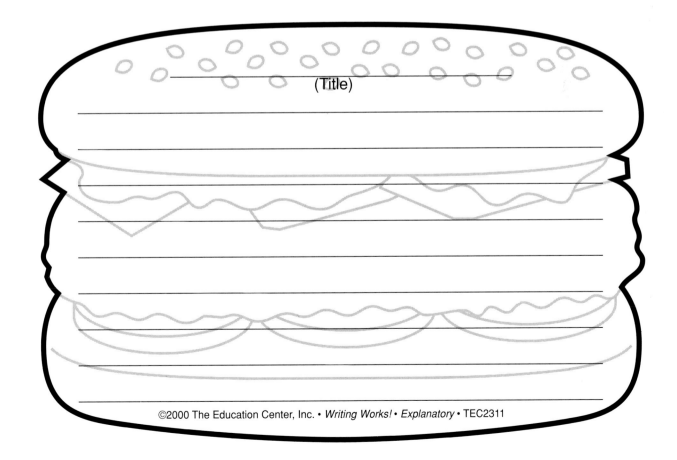

_____(Title)_____

©2000 The Education Center, Inc. • *Writing Works!* • Explanatory • TEC2311

Prepare to Perform!

PROMPT

Imagine that your class is going to put on a play about a favorite fairy tale or folktale. Write one or more paragraphs for your classmates explaining how you should prepare for this play.

Think It!

1. Have students think about the last play they participated in or saw. Ask student volunteers to explain what had to (or what they think had to) be done to prepare for it. For example, preparations might include casting characters, practicing lines, creating costumes, or making props.

2. Read aloud the prompt above, display it on a transparency, or write it on the board.

3. Give each student one copy of page 27. Have the student think of a favorite fairy tale or folktale. Direct the student to use the reproducible to help her organize her thoughts and ideas about the play preparations.

Write It!

1. On another sheet of paper, have the student use the information recorded on page 27 to write one or more paragraphs explaining how to prepare for the class play. Remind the student that she is writing to explain and should use transitional or linking words. Also remind the student to include a topic sentence and a concluding sentence in her paragraph(s).

2. Direct the student to proofread and edit her work carefully. Encourage students to swap papers to peer-edit.

3. After all corrections have been made, have the student write her final copy on a separate sheet of paper.

4. If desired, give each student a 12" x 18" sheet of light-colored construction paper. Direct the student to fold the paper in half; then draw and color a picture of an imaginary scene from the play on the front side of the paper. Then have the student glue her final writing to the inside. Display students' final copies alongside the book version of the tale. Title the display "Prepared to Perform!"

Name____________________ *Explanatory writing*

Prepare to Perform!

____

(Title of Play)

Cast	Costumes	Props

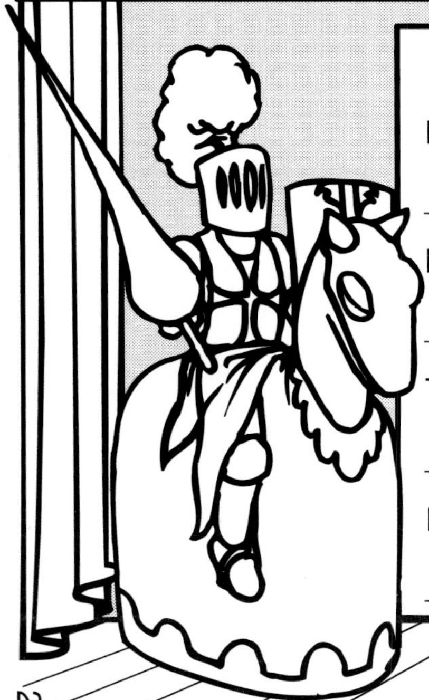

Steps to Prepare for the Play

First, ______________________

____

Next, ______________________

____

Then, ______________________

____

Finally, ______________________

____

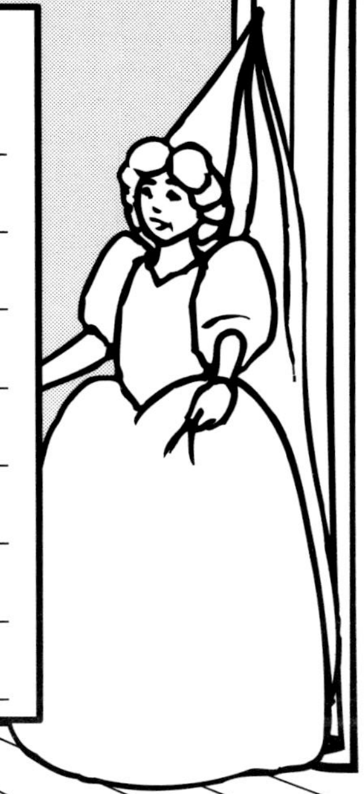

There's No Place Like Home!

PROMPT

Imagine that you are going to ride a different bus home from school. Write a paragraph for the bus driver explaining how to get to your home.

Think It!

1. Share with students the route you take to get from school to your house each day. Use directional words—such as north, south, right, or left—and include landmarks—such as special buildings or colorful houses—to help students visualize your directions. Then ask students what would happen if you were giving someone these directions and you left out one of the steps.

2. Direct each student to close his eyes and visualize the route from school to his home. Then read aloud the prompt above, display it on a transparency, or write it on the board.

3. Give each student a copy of page 29. In the first column on the chart, instruct the student to list all of the streets the bus driver will need to turn onto to get from the school to his home. In the second and third columns, challenge the student to write directional words the bus driver will need to know to turn onto each street and any landmarks she will see.

4. Instruct the student to use the information in the chart to help him write directions on the house shape explaining how to get to his home from school.

Write It!

1. On another sheet of paper, have the student use the information recorded on the reproducible to write a paragraph explaining how to get from school to his home. Remind the student that he is writing to explain and should use transitional or linking words. Also remind him to include a topic sentence and a concluding sentence in his paragraph.

2. Direct the student to proofread and edit his work carefully. Encourage students to swap papers to peer-edit. After all corrections have been made, direct the student to write his final copy on another sheet of paper.

3. If desired, give each student a 9" x 12" sheet of construction paper. On one side have the student draw and color a picture of his home; then have him glue his final copy onto the other side. Using a length of string, hang each student's picture from the ceiling and label the display "There's No Place Like Home!"

There's No Place Like Home!

Name of the Street	Direction to Turn	Helpful Landmarks

First, _____

_____

_____

Next, _____

_____

Then, _____

_____

_____

Finally, _____

_____

_____

Time for a Treat!

PROMPT

Imagine that your class has won an ice-cream sundae party. Write a paragraph to your teacher explaining how to make your sundae the way you like it.

Think It!

1. Brainstorm with students different ice-cream flavors and toppings. List student responses on the board.

2. Read aloud the prompt above, display it on a transparency, or write it on the board. Then give each student a copy of page 31.

3. In the empty ice-cream dish, have each student draw the sundae she would like her teacher to make for her. Have the student label each of the items she includes, so it is clear what ingredients are needed.

Write It!

1. Have each student review the diagram of her sundae. Then, on another sheet of paper, instruct her to write the steps needed to make her sundae. Instruct the student to number the steps in the order in which her sundae should be prepared.

2. On the same sheet of paper, have the student use the steps to write a paragraph on how to make her sundae. Remind the student she is writing to explain and should use transitional or linking words. Also remind the student to include a topic sentence and a concluding sentence in her paragraph.

3. Direct the student to proofread and edit her work carefully. Encourage students to swap papers to peer-edit.

4. After all corrections have been made, have the student write her final copy on the sundae pattern on the bottom of page 31.

5. If desired, have student volunteers read their sundae-making instructions to the class. As each student reads her instructions, direct the rest of the class to sketch the sundae being described. Then allow students to compare the picture of the original sundae with the sketches to check the accuracy of the directions.

Time for a Treat!

My Sundae

Draw your favorite sundae and label its parts.

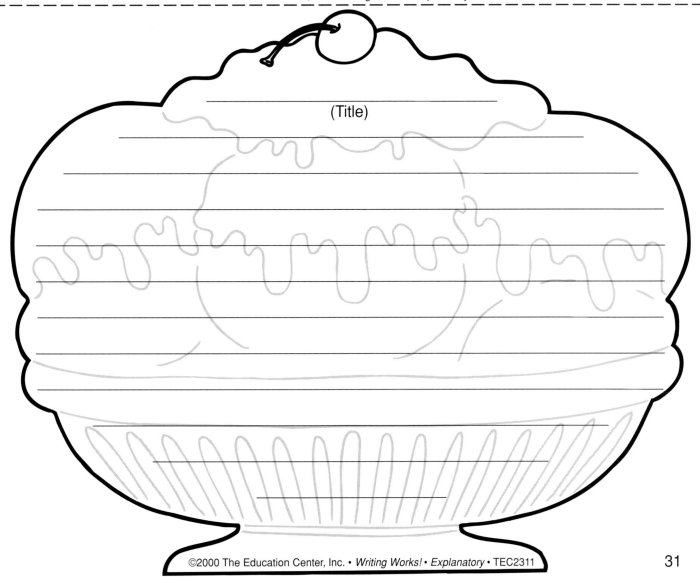

_____
(Title)

Ready, Set, Eat!

Think It!

1. Ask students if they have ever set a table. Allow student volunteers to share the steps they followed and the items they needed—such as placemats, silverware, and condiments—to set the table.

2. Read aloud the prompt above, display it on a transparency, or write it on the board.

3. Give each student a copy of page 33. Direct the student to use the top of the page to write the items he will need in order to set the table.

4. At the bottom of page 33, have the student write the steps needed to set the table correctly.

Write It!

1. On a separate sheet of paper, have the student use the information recorded on page 33 to write a paragraph to his friend explaining how to set the table. Remind the student that he is writing to explain and should use transitional or linking words. Also remind him to include a topic sentence and a concluding sentence in his paragraph.

2. Direct the student to proofread and edit his work carefully. Encourage students to swap papers to peer-edit. After all corrections have been made, instruct the student to write his final draft on another sheet of paper.

3. If desired, allow each student to glue his final draft onto a paper plate. Then display the plates on a bulletin board with a tablecloth background, and title it "Ready, Set, Eat!"

Ready, Set, Eat!

Items Needed to Set the Table

First, _____

_____

_____

Next, _____

_____

Then, _____

_____

Finally, _____

_____

_____

Student for Hire!

PROMPT *Imagine that you want to find a job in your neighborhood to earn some extra money. Think about the job that you will do. Write a paragraph explaining the steps you will need to take in order to get this job.*

PAINT

Think It!

1. Ask students to name some of the jobs students their age can do to raise money. For example, they could run a lemonade stand, mow lawns, baby-sit, help paint fences, or wash cars.

2. Discuss with students the types of things they should consider when preparing for a job. For example, they should think about what supplies they will need, any safety issues that may be involved, when they will do the job and how often, and how much they will charge.

3. Read aloud the prompt above, display it on a transparency, or write it on the board. Then give each student a copy of page 35.

4. Direct the student to use the reproducible to help her organize her thoughts and ideas for planning her job.

Write It!

1. On another sheet of paper, have the student use the information recorded on page 35 to write one or more paragraphs about how she plans to get a job to raise money. Remind her that she is writing to explain and should use transitional and linking words. Also remind her to include a topic sentence and a concluding sentence in her paragraph(s).

2. Direct the student to proofread and edit her work carefully. Encourage students to swap papers to peer-edit. After all corrections have been made, have the student write her final draft on a separate sheet of paper.

3. If desired, cover a bulletin board with classified ads from the newspaper. Post students' final drafts on the board. Title it "Students for Hire!"

Student for Hire!

Lemonade 25¢

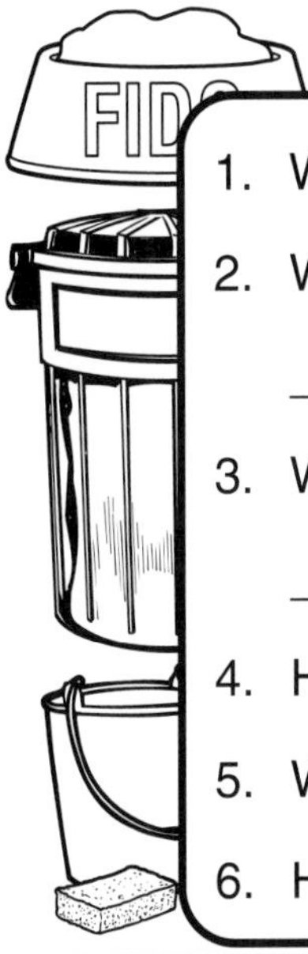

1. What job will I do? _____

2. What supplies will I need? _____

   _____

3. What safety issues should I be concerned about? _____

   _____

4. How much time will the job take? _____

5. When will I do the job? _____

6. How much will I charge? _____

Steps to Take to Get My Job:

First, _____

_____

_____

Next, _____

_____

_____

Then, _____

_____

_____

Finally, _____

_____

_____

Math Made Easy

PROMPT

Imagine that you have been asked to explain to a classmate how to solve a math problem. Write a paragraph giving detailed instructions explaining how to solve this problem.

$$6{,}000 - 593$$

$$362 \times 79$$

Think It!

1. Ask students to think about the first time they learned how to add, subtract, multiply, or divide. Point out how important it was for them to get clear directions when learning the math operations.

2. Read aloud the prompt above, display it on a transparency, or write it on the board. Then give each student a copy of page 37.

3. At the top of page 37, have the student write a challenging math problem, such as a word problem, multiplying a double-digit number by a double-digit number, or subtracting with zeros.

4. Below this, have the student list the steps needed to solve the problem. Then have him number the steps in the order in which they should be followed.

Write It!

1. On another sheet of paper, have the student use the information recorded on page 37 to write a paragraph on how to solve his problem. Remind the student that he is writing to explain and should include transitional or linking words. Also remind him to include a topic sentence and a concluding sentence in his paragraph.

2. Direct the student to proofread and edit his work carefully. Encourage students to swap papers to peer-edit.

3. After all corrections have been made, have the student write his final draft in the space provided on page 37.

4. If desired, allow each student to cut out his final draft and exchange his paper with a partner to test the directions. Then display them on a bulletin board titled "Math Made Easy."

Name _____

Math Made Easy

_____
(Title)

| | | | | | | | | | | | | |
(lined writing area)

Problem to Solve:

Steps for Solving the Problem:

Wishing Our Chores Away

PROMPT *Imagine that you have been granted one wish by a genie. You tell the genie that you would like him to do your least favorite household chore. Write a paragraph for the genie, explaining how to do your chore correctly.*

Think It!

1. Share with students your least favorite household chore and why you dislike it. Ask student volunteers to share their least favorite chore and what they dislike about it. For example, a student might say she dislikes vacuuming because her house is all carpeted and it takes her a long time to complete the chore.

2. Read aloud the prompt above, display it on a transparency, or write it on the board. Then give each student a copy of page 39.

3. At the top of page 39, have the student list the steps the genie will need to follow to successfully complete the chore.

4. Instruct the student to read over what she has written and number her steps in the order in which they should be completed.

Write It!

1. On another sheet of paper, have the student use the information on page 39 to write a paragraph explaining how to complete her least favorite chore. Remind the student that she is writing to explain and should use transitional or linking words. Also remind her to include a topic sentence and a concluding sentence in her paragraph.

2. Direct the student to proofread and edit her paper carefully. Encourage students to swap papers to peer-edit.

3. After all corrections have been made, instruct the student to write her final draft in the space provided on page 39. Then have students cut out their final drafts along the bold line.

4. If desired, in advance, ask students to bring in cleaned small plastic soda bottles. Have each student decorate her "magic wishing bottle" with arts-and-crafts supplies. Then have her roll up her final draft and put it into the bottle, leaving enough of the paper sticking out for someone to be able to get it to read. Display the bottles, then title the display "Wishing Our Chores Away."

Wishing Our Chores Away

Steps to Complete My Chore

_____
_____
_____
_____
_____
_____
_____
_____

_____
(Title)
_____
_____
_____
_____
_____
_____
_____
_____
_____
_____

Report Roundup

PROMPT

Imagine that you have been assigned to teach a younger student how to give an oral report. Write a paragraph to this student explaining the steps he or she will need to follow in order to prepare for this report.

Think It!

1. Have students think about a time when they gave an oral report.

2. Ask student volunteers to share the topic of a particular report they gave, such as animal habitats, a famous person, or a specific book. Then have them tell about the things they did to prepare for giving this report. For example, a student might say he had to research the topic, take notes, write his speech, and make a visual aid. List student responses on the board.

3. Read aloud the prompt above, display it on a transparency, or write it on the board. Then give each student a copy of page 41.

4. Assign each student a different report topic or have him choose one. Instruct the student to fill in the space provided on the reproducible with the materials and steps needed to prepare for his report. Then have him read over his steps and number them in the correct order.

Write It!

1. On another sheet of paper, challenge the student to use the information recorded on page 41 to write a paragraph explaining how he plans to prepare for his report. Remind the student that he is writing to explain and should use transitional or linking words. Also remind him to include a topic sentence and a concluding sentence in his paragraph.

2. Direct the student to proofread and edit his work carefully. Encourage students to swap papers to peer-edit.

3. After all corrections have been made, instruct the student to write his final version on another sheet of paper.

4. If desired, have each student glue his final writing onto a 9" x 12" sheet of construction paper. Bind the students' sheets together in a book titled "Report Roundup."

Report Roundup

Steps for Preparing the Report:

Materials Needed for the Report:

Name _____

41

Author Interviews

PROMPT *Imagine that you have the chance to meet and interview your favorite author. Write one or more paragraphs explaining the steps you would take to conduct the interview.*

Think It!

1. Ask student volunteers to share a time when they saw an interview on TV. Have them explain how well they thought the interviewer conducted the interview.

2. Review with students proper interviewing techniques, such as getting materials ready ahead of time, making the guest comfortable, asking thoughtful questions, and closing the interview. Mention the types of questions that would be appropriate to ask and those that wouldn't be. For example, it is impolite to ask how much money someone makes.

3. Read aloud the prompt above, display it on a transparency, or write it on the board. Then give each student a copy of page 43.

4. Challenge the student to think about how she would conduct an interview with her favorite author. Direct the student to use page 43 to help her organize her thoughts and ideas.

Write It!

1. On another sheet of paper, have the student use the information recorded on the reproducible to write one or more paragraphs explaining how to conduct an interview. Remind the student that she is writing to explain and should use transitional or linking words. Also remind her to include a topic and a concluding sentence in her paragraph(s).

2. Direct the student to proofread and edit her work carefully. Encourage students to swap papers to peer-edit. After all corrections have been made, instruct the student to write her final copy on a separate sheet of paper.

3. If desired, allow each student to conduct a mock interview with a classmate. Direct one student to conduct the interview, while the other student pretends to be the author. Then instruct them to trade places and repeat the process.

Author Interviews

Which author will I interview?

_____

Where will I conduct the interview?

_____

When will I conduct the interview?

_____

What materials will I need?

_____

_____

What questions will I ask?

_____

_____

_____

_____

_____

What steps will I follow to conduct the interview?

First, _____

_____

Next, _____

_____

Then, _____

_____

Finally, _____

_____

Name_____

Proofreading Checklist

To the Student: Use this checklist during the proofreading or editing stage of your writing to help you determine what needs improving and/or correcting before writing the final version. Then give this checklist and your writing to a peer editor (a classmate) to use to edit your work.

Title of Writing Selection:_____

Things to Check	Writer's Checklist		Peer Editor's Checklist	
	Yes	No	Yes	No
1. Does the writing have a topic sentence and a concluding sentence?				
2. Does the writing explain how to do something in a logical order? Are any steps omitted?				
3. Is the reader able to understand how to complete the task explained?				
4. Does the writing make sense and is it easy to read?				
5. Did the writer use details that help explain the steps?				
6. Did the writer use transitional words such as *first, next, then,* and *finally*?				
7. Does each sentence begin with a capital letter?				
8. Does each sentence have an ending punctuation mark?				
9. Did the writer use complete sentences?				
10. Did the writer check for misspelled words?				
11. Is each paragraph indented?				

☆ If the peer editor checked "No" in any box above, discuss it with the editor.

Think About It!

I think I did a _____ job on this writing selection because…

_____

_____

Explanatory-Writing Assessment

Student's Name: _____ **Date:** _____

Title of Writing: _____

Assessment Items	Agree	Disagree
1. The writing selection has a topic sentence and concluding sentence.		
2. The writing selection explains how to do something.		
3. The writing selection shows a logical order in the steps of the explanation.		
4. The writing selection makes sense; it is easy to read.		
5. Specific details are used to enhance the explained steps.		
6. All details relate to the topic.		
7. Descriptive words and details are used.		
8. Transitional words such as *first, next, then,* and *finally* are used.		
9. Correct punctuation and capitalization are used.		
10. Each word is spelled correctly.		
11. Run-on sentences and incomplete sentences are avoided.		
12. Each verb agrees with its subject.		
13. All proper nouns are capitalized.		
14. Each paragraph is indented.		
15. Apostrophes are correctly used to form contractions and to show possession.		

Comments: _____

_____

_____

_____

_____

©2000 The Education Center, Inc. • *Writing Works!* • Explantory • TEC2311   45

Extra Prompts

1. Who doesn't love getting a gift on her birthday? Write a paragraph explaining how to wrap a beautiful gift for someone's birthday.

2. Ever heard someone say, "It's as easy as riding a bike"? Well, just how easy is it? Write a paragraph explaining how to ride a bike.

3. Most everyone has experienced severe weather from time to time, such as a thunderstorm, hurricane, or blizzard. What kind of severe weather have you and your family experienced? Write a report to your family explaining how to prepare for a particular type of storm.

4. Cleaning a bedroom is such a chore! Write a paragraph to a friend explaining the best way to do this.

5. Your mom or dad has asked you to teach your little brother or sister how to properly answer the phone. Write a paragraph explaining how to do this.

6. Ah, the thought of a picnic on a perfect summer day. Imagine that you've invited a friend on a picnic. Then write a letter to your friend explaining how you will prepare for this event.

7. It's almost time for your six-month dental checkup. Your dentist calls you and asks that you be prepared to explain how to correctly brush your teeth! Write a note to your dentist explaining how to do this.

8. Imagine that you and a friend are attending a cool school dance. Your friend would like to learn a new dance for the occasion. Write a set of instructions that you'll use to teach your friend a new dance.

Extra Prompts

9. Imagine that you're preparing for a bubble-blowing contest. Write a paragraph explaining how to blow the biggest bubble with chewing gum.

10. Who ever said that you can't teach an old dog a new trick? Write a letter to the American Kennel Club explaining how to teach a dog a trick.

11. Who doesn't like to make new friends? Imagine that you are going on the radio to tell people how to do this. Write a paragraph explaining what you'd say.

12. Washing a car is a great way to earn extra money. Write an advertisement that includes an explanation of how to wash a car.

13. Your best friend wants advice on how to study for a test. Write a note to your friend explaining how to do this.

14. It's your turn to clean up the dinner dishes, but you have been invited to eat at a friend's house. Your little brother has volunteered to do the dishes for you. Write a note to your brother explaining how to do this.

15. Your mom has asked your older cousin to drive you to the grocery store. Your cousin doesn't know how to get to the store. Write a paragraph for your cousin explaining how to get from your house to the grocery store.

16. You and your family are going on vacation. Your little sister wrote you a note telling you that she doesn't know how to pack a suitcase! Write a response to your sister explaining how to do this.

Editing Symbols

Writers use special marks called *editing symbols* to help them edit and revise their work. Editing symbols are used to show what changes a writer wants to make in his or her writing.

Symbol	Meaning	Example
⬯	Correct spelling.	(animl)
ℓ	Delete or remove.	dogg
⌒	Close the gap.	fi sh
∧	Add a letter or word.	lives in tree a
#	Make a space.	fliessouth
∽	Reverse the order of a letter, a word, or words.	plants eats
⟨,⟩	Insert a comma.	the crab an arthropod
⊙	Insert a period.	Cats purr
⋁	Insert an apostrophe.	a deers antlers
⋎ ⋎	Insert quotation marks.	She said, Look at the pig.
≡	Make the letter a capital.	birds eat seeds.
/	Make the letter lowercase.	a Snowshoe hare
¶	Start a new paragraph.	¶Some dogs have tails.

©2000 The Education Center, Inc. • *Writing Works!* • *Explanatory* • TEC2311